CONTENTS

D1406553

Pack It Up

The LaRose family is taking a trip through the United States starting from their home in Seattle, Washington. Today Mom, Dad, Judi, and Peter are packing up their minivan, the Blue Torpedo.

A sentence is a group of words that tells a complete thought. A sentence has a subject and a predicate. The **subject** names someone or something. The **predicate** tells what the subject does. This is a sentence: *Dogs bark*.

If a group of words lacks either a subject or a predicate, it is not a sentence. *Chases the squirrels* has no subject. It is not a sentence.

Read the groups of words. Write *sentence* or *not a sentence* after each item.

1. Our tent is blue and red. _____

2. My toothpaste and washcloth. _____

3. We need bathing suits and sandals. _____

4. Peter has four rolls of film. _____

5. Mom's sunglasses. _____

6. Putting gas in the minivan. _____

7. Have to get up early in the morning. _____

8. The juice and crackers are in the cooler. _____

9. Judi packs her suitcase. _____

10. In the back with the sleeping bags. _____

Go for It!

Imagine you are taking a trip. Describe where you're going and what you expect to see. Make sure all your sentences are complete.

Know What?

Pioneers from Illinois founded a settlement along Puget Sound in 1851. They named their new town Seattle after Chief Sealth, a Duwamish Indian who had become their friend.

Subject and Predicate

To compare whole numbers, look at the same-place digits in each number starting on the left.

Example: 56   72
↑   ↑
more tens
56 < 72

50 is less than 70.
So 56 is less than 72.
56 < 72

You can compare numbers with symbols.

Words	Symbol	Example
is equal to	=	56 = 56
is less than	<	56 < 72
is greater than	>	72 > 56

The LaRose family forgot to pack some things for the trip. So they are shopping in Spokane. Look at the ads for the two stores. Compare the prices.

Write the prices on the lines. Write <, =, or > in the boxes.

	Spokane Sport		Spokane Supermart
1. backpack	_____		_____
2. cooler	_____		_____
3. binoculars	_____		_____
4. camp stove	_____		_____
5. tent	_____		_____
TOTAL	_____		_____

Spokane SPORT
tent $127
binoculars $87
cooler $31
camp stove $68
backpack $27

6. The LaRose family wants to go to only one store. Which one should they choose to save money?

_____

7. How much will they save? _____

Spokane SUPERMART
backpack $19
camp stove $79
tent $108
cooler $27
binoculars $89

Go for It!

Look at some newspaper advertisements. Compare prices at two stores. Choose three items sold at both stores. How much money can you save?

Know What?

Washington is the only state named after a U.S. president.

Compare Numbers/Operational Symbols

Let's Float

Hells Canyon on the Idaho-Oregon border is the deepest canyon in North America. Its deepest spot is more than 7,000 feet. The canyon is a popular place for river rafting.

Why does a rubber raft float in a river? Because of **buoyancy** (**boy**-uhn-see). Buoyancy is the force of water pushing on an object. Things that are light compared to their size float. Things that are heavy compared to their size sink.

The comparison of size to weight is called **density**. Water has a density of 1. Anything with a density less than 1 will float. Anything with a density greater than 1 will sink.

The family's raft has tipped over. Here are some things from their boat. Draw ↑ in the bubble next to each object that will float. Draw ↓ in the bubble near each object that will sink. (Hint: Look at the objects' densities: <1 means less than 1 and >1 means greater than 1.)

>1

<1

<1

<1

Dad's sunglasses _____ because their density is

_____ than the density of water.

Buoyancy and Density

Go for It!

Plan a rafting trip. Draw a map of a river and show your route. Put in people, animals, trees, and other things you might see.

Know What?

Daredevil rider Evel Knievel tried to jump the Snake River Canyon on a rocket-powered motorcycle in 1974. But he did not make it to the other side. His parachute opened too early, and he floated safely to the ground.

Buoyancy and Density

Montana is the fourth largest state in the United States. Western Montana has tall, rugged mountains with forests and mines. Eastern Montana, with its open plains, has the nickname Big Sky Country.

The LaRose family is driving through Montana. They notice on the map that the distance from Missoula to Montana's capital, Helena, is about 112 miles. You can write 112 in expanded notation: 112 = 100 + 10 + 2.

Write these distances in Montana in expanded notation.

1. 48 = _____

2. 120 = _____

3. 125 = _____

4. 236 = _____

5. 79 = _____

6. 261 = _____

7. 435 = _____

8. 372 = _____

9. 303 = _____

10. 197 = _____

Go for It!

Write the numbers above in expanded notation, but use words instead of numerals. For example, 112 = one hundred + ten + two.

Know What?

Montana's Glacier National Park, with more than 50 glaciers and 200 lakes, is on the Continental Divide. The rivers on the west side flow to the Pacific. The rivers on the east side flow to the Atlantic and the Gulf of Mexico.

Expanded Notation

Natural Treasures

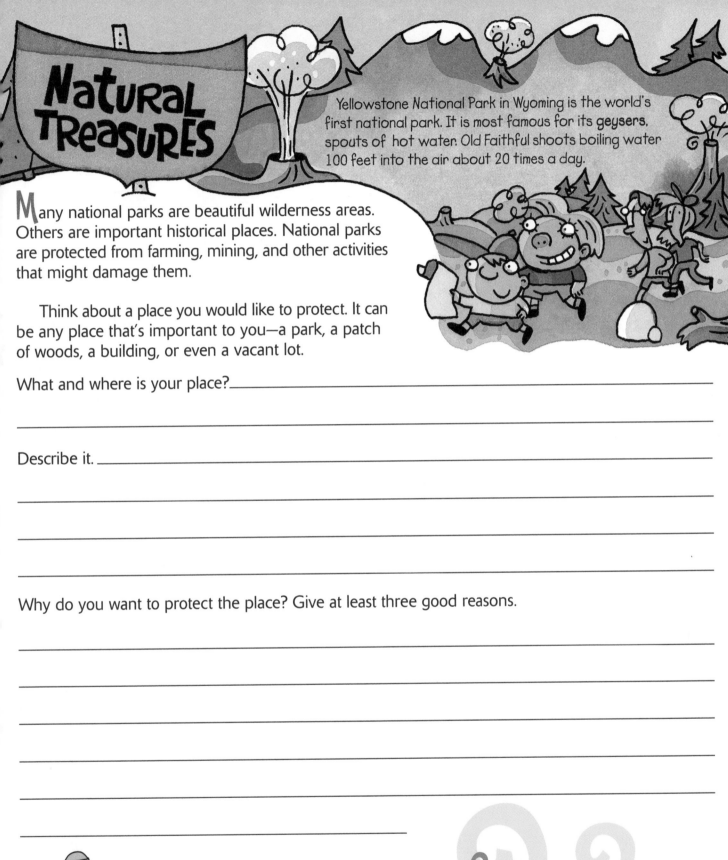

Yellowstone National Park in Wyoming is the world's first national park. It is most famous for its geysers, spouts of hot water. Old Faithful shoots boiling water 100 feet into the air about 20 times a day.

Many national parks are beautiful wilderness areas. Others are important historical places. National parks are protected from farming, mining, and other activities that might damage them.

Think about a place you would like to protect. It can be any place that's important to you—a park, a patch of woods, a building, or even a vacant lot.

What and where is your place? _____

_____

Describe it. _____

_____

_____

_____

Why do you want to protect the place? Give at least three good reasons.

_____

_____

_____

_____

_____

Go for It!
Choose a national park you would like to visit. Write to the park for information about it.

Q: What is full of holes but still holds water?

A: A sponge!

Descriptive and Persuasive Sentences

Dakota Addition

In South Dakota, farms and ranches cover about 9/10 of the land. There are lots of wheat fields and huge herds of beef cattle.

SUM
the answer to an addition problem

The LaRose family is visiting South Dakota's best-known attraction.

Write the sums. Then write the letter next to each sum to decode the message.

$$\begin{array}{r} 33 \\ + 4 \\ \hline \end{array}$$
O

$$\begin{array}{r} 25 \\ +16 \\ \hline \end{array}$$
U

$$\begin{array}{r} 99 \\ 2 \\ + 3 \\ \hline \end{array}$$
T

$$\begin{array}{r} 49 \\ 5 \\ +60 \\ \hline \end{array}$$
S

$$\begin{array}{r} 10 \\ 15 \\ +11 \\ \hline \end{array}$$
R

$$\begin{array}{r} 34 \\ 28 \\ +17 \\ \hline \end{array}$$
E

$$\begin{array}{r} 72 \\ 9 \\ + 8 \\ \hline \end{array}$$
N

$$\begin{array}{r} 10 \\ 0 \\ + 7 \\ \hline \end{array}$$
H

$$\begin{array}{r} 12 \\ 25 \\ +29 \\ \hline \end{array}$$
M

Where are Judi and Peter? __ __ __ __ __   __ __ __ __ __ __ __ __
66 37 41 89 104   36 41 114 17 66 37 36 79

 Go for It!

Play this addition game with a friend. Make a deck of 40 cards using the numbers 0 to 19 twice. Mix the cards up and place them facedown. Take turns drawing any two cards and saying the sum. If the sum is right, the player takes the cards. If it is wrong, the player returns the cards to the deck. The player with the most matches when the deck is used up wins.

Know What?
The Homestead Mine, opened in 1876, is the oldest continuously operating gold mine in the world. It's located in the town of Lead in the Black Hills.

Addition Facts (Two-Digit Numbers)

MEGA MALL

The Mall of America in Bloomington, Minnesota, is one of the biggest shopping malls in the world. It has more than 400 stores, an indoor amusement park called Camp Snoopy, and an aquarium complete with sharks.

Parts of speech are words that do jobs in sentences. Nouns name people, places, or things. Verbs tell what nouns do. Adjectives tell more about nouns, and adverbs describe verbs and adjectives. Adverbs often end in *-ly*.

The thirsty shoppers slurped their smoothies sloppily.

adjective — VERB — adverb — NOUN — NOUN

Read the paragraph. Identify the part of speech of each underlined word. Write the verbs in Mom's shopping bag, the adjectives in Dad's, the adverbs in Judi's, and the nouns in Peter's.

Camp Snoopy at the Mall of America is a <u>big</u> indoor amusement park. The <u>park</u> looks like it is outdoors. The <u>sun</u> <u>shines</u> <u>brightly</u> through skylights. About 400 <u>tall</u> <u>trees</u> and 30,000 plants <u>grow</u> in the park. Sometimes, insects <u>attack</u> these plants. So gardeners have let 20,000 <u>ladybugs</u> loose in the park. The hungry ladybugs <u>quickly</u> <u>gobble</u> up the <u>harmful</u> insects.

Verbs

Nouns

Adjectives

Adverbs

Go for It!

Choose an interesting article from an old newspaper. After you read it, circle the nouns. Underline the verbs. Draw a box around the adjectives. Draw a line through the adverbs. Which parts of speech did you notice most? Why do you think that is?

Know What?

Workers brought in 55 semi-truckloads of black dirt so that the plants and trees at Camp Snoopy could grow.

Parts of Speech

GREAT Lakes

Lake Superior is the world's largest freshwater lake. It is the largest, deepest, and cleanest of the five Great Lakes that share part of the border between the United States and Canada.

The LaRose family is traveling around Lake Superior. Find each difference and write it in the blank. Then write the differences next to the cities near Lake Superior. You will see which way the LaRoses went.

1. 27 – 18 = _____ Ironwood

2. 136 – 119 = _____ Ashland

3. 285 – 283 = _____ Sault Ste. Marie (U.S.)

4. 276 – 190 = _____ Thunder Bay

5. 179 – 21 = _____ Nipigon

6. 158 – 39 = _____ Sault Ste. Marie (Canada)

7. 81 – 27 = _____ Superior

8. 91 – 83 = _____ Copper Harbor

9. 52 – 49 = _____ Marquette

COOL WORD

DIFFERENCE
the answer to a subtraction problem

Nipigon

Thunder Bay

Canada
U.S.A.

Lake Superior

Sault Ste. Marie

Copper Harbor

Sault Ste. Marie

Marquette

Superior

Ashland

Ironwood

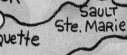

Go for It!

Write two story problems using subtraction facts. Write a "take-away" story and a story comparing two different things.

Know What?

Whitefish Bay is known as a graveyard for ships. In 1975, the *Edmund Fitzgerald*, a 726-foot supership, along with its 29-man crew, sank without a trace. The wreck was found off Whitefish Point. Some people believe that the pressure on the ship from huge swells of water made it break in half.

Subtraction Facts (Two- and Three-Digit Numbers)

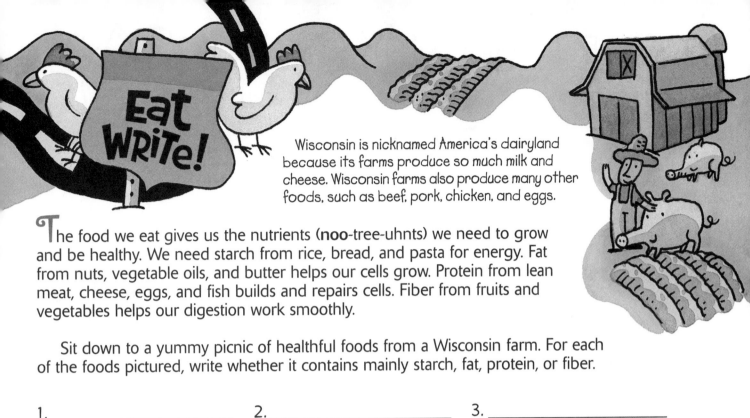

Eat WRiTe!

Wisconsin is nicknamed America's dairyland because its farms produce so much milk and cheese. Wisconsin farms also produce many other foods, such as beef, pork, chicken, and eggs.

The food we eat gives us the nutrients (**noo**-tree-uhnts) we need to grow and be healthy. We need starch from rice, bread, and pasta for energy. Fat from nuts, vegetable oils, and butter helps our cells grow. Protein from lean meat, cheese, eggs, and fish builds and repairs cells. Fiber from fruits and vegetables helps our digestion work smoothly.

Sit down to a yummy picnic of healthful foods from a Wisconsin farm. For each of the foods pictured, write whether it contains mainly starch, fat, protein, or fiber.

1. _____

2. _____

3. _____

4. _____

5. _____

6. _____

Go for It!

Make a food group poster. Cut out pictures of foods from grocery store advertisements. Write *Starches*, *Proteins*, *Fats*, and *Fiber* as headings on a large sheet of paper. Paste the pictures in the correct columns. Hang your poster in the kitchen.

Q. What did the grape say when the elephant stepped on it?

A. Nothing, it just let out a little whine (wine)!

Food Groups

Chicago is...

Chicago is the third largest city in the United States. Chicago is famous for its skyscrapers and also for museums, parks, sports teams, blues music, and, of course, stuffed pizza!

We use four main types of sentences.

- A **statement** tells something. *Chicago's nickname is the Windy City.*
- A **question** asks something. *What is on the menu at Michael Jordan's restaurant?*
- A **command** gives an order. *Don't forget to buy tickets.*
- An **exclamation** expresses a strong feeling. *How expensive everything is!*

Identify the sentences in the picture. Write *s* in the box if the sentence is a statement. Write *q* if the sentence is a question. Write *c* if the sentence is a command. Write *e* if the sentence is an exclamation.

Stop.

Who wants pizza?

What a huge fountain!

The dolphins and beluga whales leaped into the air.

Go for It!

Write a command, a statement, an exclamation, and a question. Use a different word below in each sentence.

drive   skyscraper   basketball   buy

Types of Sentences

Types of Sentences

Let's RACE!

Indiana has steel mills and oil refineries near Gary as well as rolling farmland in Brown County. Indianapolis, its capital and largest city, is known for the Indy 500 automobile race, which is held on Memorial Day.

Speed around the race track as you find each sum.

COOL WORD

ADDENDS are the numbers to be added. In 43 + 57 = 100, 43 and 57 are the addends.

START

```
 43
+ 56
```

```
 29
+ 15
```

```
 150
+ 28
```

```
 298
 429
+ 409
```

```
 46
+ 29
```

```
 346
 713
+ 187
```

```
 373
+ 218
```

```
 406
+ 35
```

```
 183
+ 671
```

```
 340
+ 420
```

Pit

Go for It!

There are many different addition problems that have a sum of 100. Think of at least 10 addition problems with two-digit addends that add up to 100.

Know What?

The first long-distance automobile race on a track in the United States took place on May 30, 1911, at the Indianapolis Motor Speedway. Ray Harroun won the 500-mile race, averaging a speed of about 75 miles per hour.

Addition Facts (Three-Digit Numbers)

A Hall of Fame

Ohio is called the "Buckeye State" after the many buckeye trees that once grew here. One of Ohio's many interesting places to visit is the Pro Football Hall of Fame in Canton.

A **common noun** names any person, place, or thing. A **proper noun** names a particular person, place, or thing. Proper nouns begin with capital letters.

Common Nouns	Proper Nouns
person	Judi
month	April
place	Beech Street
state	Ohio

The paragraph below has several mistakes. Draw this mark ≡ under letters that should be capitalized. Draw this mark ∕ through letters that should not be capitalized. Hint: remember that sentences begin with capital letters.

Example: judi and Peter went to the football Ǥame.

The Stars of football shine at the Pro Football Hall of Fame in canton, ohio. the Hall of Fame opened on september 7, 1963. Every year, the league names a few of its Best players to the Hall of Fame. there, visitors can See pictures of these players, their Uniforms, and their equipment.

Go for It!

Write the name of your favorite athlete. If the athlete plays for a team, write the name of the team and the team's home city. Make sure you use capital letters in the right places.

Q: Why wasn't Cinderella good at football?

A: Because her coach was a pumpkin!

Common and Proper Nouns

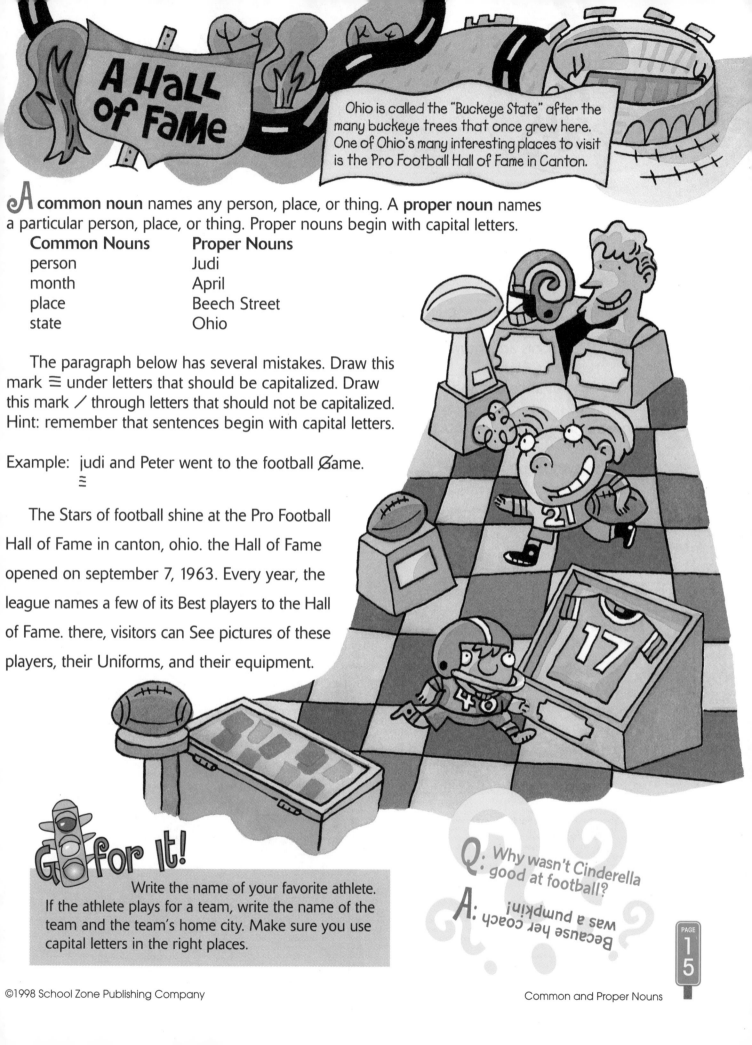

Map the Falls

Niagara Falls, one of North America's most famous attractions, lies on the Niagara River between Lake Erie and Lake Ontario. Half of the falls lies in the United States and half lies in Canada. Horseshoe Falls is in Canada. American Falls is in the U. S.

A map is a special kind of picture. Maps give information about an area using lines, colors, shapes, and other symbols. These symbols show where roads, cities, rivers, lakes, and many other things are located. The part of a map that tells what the symbols mean is called the **key** or **legend**.

Use the map and key to answer the questions.

1. How many power plants are shown on the map? _____

2. What is the name of the big island? _____

3. About how many miles wide is it?_____

4. What does this symbol mean? 🏙 _____

5. How many lakes are shown on the map? _____

6. What are their names? _____

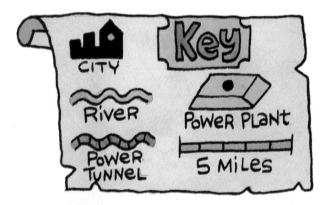

Go for It!

Hide a treat somewhere around your house. Draw a map showing where the treat is hidden. Use symbols and include a legend to explain what your symbols mean. Ask a friend to use your map to find the treat.

Map and Map Key

ST. LAWRENCE SEAWAY

Ships can travel from the Atlantic Ocean to the Great Lakes. They use the St. Lawrence Seaway—the St. Lawrence River, canals, and lakes.

Verbs have different forms, or **tenses**, to tell what happened, what's happening now, or what will happen. To make many verbs past tense, add the letters *-ed* to the end of the verb. *The river flowed to the sea.* To make a verb future tense, add *will* before the verb. *I will see you on the boat tomorrow.*

Write the correct tense of the word in parentheses in each blank.

1. The Seaway _____ (open) on June 26, 1959.

2. Today, ships from many countries _____ (use) the Seaway.

3. The Seaway _____ (close) every winter because of ice.

4. Improvements to the St. Lawrence Seaway _____ (continue).

5. The French _____ (construct) a canal around the St. Lawrence River in 1680.

6. Peter _____ (read) more about the St. Lawrence Seaway when he gets home.

Go for It!

Write a sentence about something you did yesterday. Then rewrite that sentence using present and future tenses.

Q: How did the rude ship's captain enter a room?

A: He barged right in!

Verb Tenses

WHaT FLoWeRS ARe foR

The Adirondack Mountains are in northeastern New York. More than 40 of the peaks in the Adirondacks rise more than 4,000 feet. The mountains are famous for their forests and hundreds of beautiful lakes.

All the parts of a flower do a different job in seed making.

- The male parts of a flower, the **stamens**, make pollen. Most plants have several stamens. The stamens are often tan.
- The female parts of the flower, the **pistil**, make ovules (**ohv**-yools). Most pistils are green.
- The colorful **corolla** is made of petals that attract birds and insects. These animals spread the pollen from one flower to the ovules of another flower so seeds can begin to form.
- The **calyx** is the outer part of the flower. It has little leaves.

Label the parts of the flower.

Why do most plants need seeds?

_____

_____

Go for It!

Make a notebook of pressed flowers. Collect some wildflowers. Put them in an old phone book or under a heavy weight. When the flowers are dry, tape them into a notebook. Look up their names and write labels to identify the flowers.

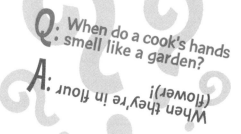

Q: When do a cook's hands smell like a garden?

A: When they're in flour (flower)!

Plant Parts

Tea Time

Many important events in America's fight for independence from England happened in Boston. The Boston Tea Party was one of them.

Writers often use words like *first*, *next*, *then*, *after*, and *later* to help readers understand the order that things happen in a story.

These sentences are out of order. Number them in the correct order. The first one is done for you.

_____ Next, they sneaked onto the British ships.

___1___ A group of British ships carrying tea arrived in Boston.

_____ However, the governor said no.

_____ When the colonists saw the ships, they asked the governor to send them back.

_____ First, they dressed up as Indians.

_____ After that, a group of colonists decided to take action.

_____ Once on the ship, they dumped the tea into the water.

Go for It!

Write about an interesting day in your life. You can write a true story or a made-up story. Use words such as *first*, *next*, *then*, and *finally* to make the order that things happen in your story clear.

Know What?

English Puritans founded Boston in 1630. They named the city after Boston, England, where they came from.

Order of Events

NEW YORK, NEW YORK

There are many tall buildings in New York City.

Match the buildings with the heights on the right. Then number the buildings from 1 to 5 to show the order of the buildings from tallest to shortest. (1 = tallest)

_____	Chrysler Building, 77 stories	1,250 feet
_____	Citicorp Center, 59 stories	915 feet
_____	Empire State Building, 102 stories	1,377 feet
_____	RCA Building, 70 stories	850 feet
_____	World Trade Center, 110 stories	1,046 feet

How much taller is the tallest building than the shortest building?

_____

_____

Know What?
The Empire State Building has 102 floors, 1,860 steps, 73 elevators, 60 miles of water pipes, and 5 acres of windows.

Comparative Relationships

New York City is made up of five parts called **boroughs**: the Bronx, Brooklyn, Manhattan, Queens, and Staten Island. Many bridges and tunnels connect the boroughs.

Bridge	Connects	Total Length
Brooklyn	Manhattan and Brooklyn	3,455 feet
George Washington	Manhattan and New Jersey	4,760 feet
Queensboro	Manhattan and Queens	3,724 feet
Verrazano-Narrows	Staten Island and Brooklyn	6,690 feet
Williamsburg	Manhattan and Brooklyn	2,793 feet

Write the name and length of each bridge.

1.  _____

2.  _____

3.  _____

4.  _____

5.  _____

Go for It!
Arrange five objects from longest to shortest or from tallest to shortest. (You may want to measure with a ruler.) Record your results in a chart or graph.

Q. Where in New York City do wild horses live?
A. The Broncs (Bronx)!

Comparative Relationships

PHILLIE LOVES PRETZELS

The Declaration of Independence was signed in Philadelphia. Philadelphia is also the country's pretzel capital. People in Philadelphia eat about 12 times more pretzels than people anywhere else in the country.

Periods are one of the most useful punctuation marks. Here are some ways periods are used:

- at the end of sentences that are statements or commands: *You can visit a pretzel factory in Philadelphia.*
- after the letters *A.M.* and *P.M.* in times: *7:00 A.M.*
- after **abbreviations**, words that are shortened: *Tues., Dec., Calif.*
- after a person's abbreviated title: *Dr. Johnson, Mrs. Minniver*

The LaRose family is visiting the Pretzel Museum in Philadelphia. Read about their pretzel adventure as you practice using periods. Put periods where they belong in the sentences.

1. The Pretzel Museum is open from Mon through Sat from 9 a m to 5 p m

2. Its address is 211 North Third St , Philadelphia

3. Mr LaRose ate six pretzels

4. America's first pretzel bakery opened in Lititz, Penn in 1861

5. The LaRose family saw a 7-min movie on pretzels

6. They bought a box of pretzels for their friend, Dr Banks

Go for It!

Periods have more uses than those listed on this page. The next time you read a book, magazine, or newspaper, pay attention to the periods. Try to find some other ways periods are used.

Know What?

Pretzels were first baked 1,300 years ago to reward children who learned their prayers. The shape of these salty treats was meant to look like arms crossed in prayer.

Punctuation: Period

Make a Time Line

Baltimore is Maryland's largest city. It lies on Chesapeake Bay. Ships from all over the world come to Baltimore to load and unload goods.

A time line is one good way to show the order of events.

Use the information in the paragraph below to fill in the blanks in this time line.

The first Europeans arrived in what is now Baltimore in 1661. In 1729, Baltimore Town was founded. Eighty-five years later, Francis Scott Key wrote "The Star Spangled Banner" as he watched the British bomb the city. The entire downtown area of Baltimore burned to the ground in the Great Baltimore Fire of 1901. Ninety-one years after that, the Baltimore Orioles baseball team got a new stadium.

| 1661 | ☐ | ☐ | 1901 | ☐ |

| | Baltimore Town founded | "Star Spangled Banner" written | | Orioles get new park |

_____

_____

_____

Go for It!

Make a time line of your life. Start when you were born and put in the most important things that have happened to you. If you like, draw a small picture showing each event.

Know What?

Cal Ripken, Jr., of the Orioles made baseball history on September 6, 1995, in Baltimore. That's when he played his 2,131st game in a row to break Lou Gehrig's record.

Time Line

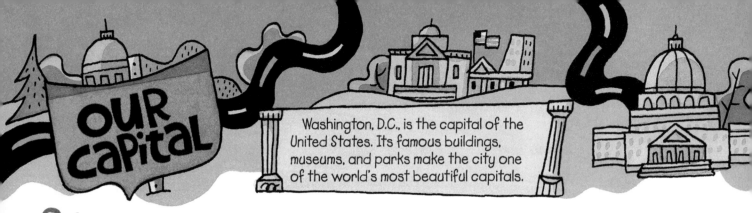

OUR CAPITAL

Washington, D.C., is the capital of the United States. Its famous buildings, museums, and parks make the city one of the world's most beautiful capitals.

Words that have opposite meanings are called **antonyms**. Words that have about the same meaning are called **synonyms**. Words that sound alike but have different spellings and meanings are called **homophones**.

Look at the words in the picture. On the line near each word pair, write *antonyms, synonyms,* or *homophones.*

short   tall

hair   hare

1. _____

2. _____

large   big

fat   skinny

3. _____

4. _____

Antonyms, Synonyms, and Homophones

5. _____

6. _____

7. _____

8. _____

9. _____

10. _____

Go for It!

Play a synonym game with a friend or two. Write some common words on slips of paper. Choose a slip. See how many synonyms you can write in one minute.

Know What?

The city of Washington, D.C., was designed by a French engineer, Pierre Charles L'Enfant. It's one of the few cities in the world that was designed before it was built.

Antonyms, Synonyms, and Homophones

Historic Virginia

Virginia is the site of many historic events. In 1607 Jamestown became the first permanent English settlement in North America. Some of the greatest battles in the Revolutionary and Civil Wars were fought here. Many tourists visit Virginia's battlefields, old churches, and colonial homes.

Visit each historic place in Virginia to find the differences.

1. Arlington
$$\begin{array}{r} 79 \\ -\ 45 \\ \hline \end{array}$$

2. Alexandria
$$\begin{array}{r} 91 \\ -\ 39 \\ \hline \end{array}$$

Washington, D.C.

3. Fredricksburg
$$\begin{array}{r} 724 \\ -\ 519 \\ \hline \end{array}$$

4. Richmond
$$\begin{array}{r} 736 \\ -\ 198 \\ \hline \end{array}$$

5. Williamsburg
$$\begin{array}{r} 600 \\ -\ 295 \\ \hline \end{array}$$

6. Jamestown
$$\begin{array}{r} 905 \\ -\ 108 \\ \hline \end{array}$$

7. Appomattox
$$\begin{array}{r} 596 \\ -\ 298 \\ \hline \end{array}$$

8. Norfolk
$$\begin{array}{r} 390 \\ -\ 64 \\ \hline \end{array}$$

Go for It!

Check your answers using addition.

Example:
$$\begin{array}{r} 75 \\ -\ 29 \\ \hline 46 \end{array}$$

Check:
$$\begin{array}{r} 46 \\ +\ 29 \\ \hline 75 \end{array}$$

Know What?

Virginia is called the "Mother of Presidents" because eight U.S. presidents were born there. They include four of the first five presidents. Can you name them? If you can't, how can you find their names?

Subtraction Facts (Three-Digit Numbers)

Mammoth Cave in Kentucky, the longest known cave system in the world, has passageways that connect more than 300 miles of caves. Underground rivers flow into dark lakes where blind fish and salamanders live.

Caves are formed when water drips through the earth and eats away a hollow in the rock underground. When the water flows away, a cave remains. Here are some parts of a cave:

- **chamber**—a large "room" in a cave
- **stalagmite**—a pointy pillar that rises from the floor
- **stalactite**—a pointy "icicle" that hangs from the ceiling
- **column**—a pillar formed when a stalactite and stalagmite join

Write the names of the cave parts on the lines.

Go for It!

Use modeling clay of various colors and a cardboard box to build a model of a cave. Make chambers, stalagmites, stalactites, and sinkholes.

Q. What do you have to watch out for when you're exploring a cave?

A: A hole (whole) lot of stuff!

Parts of a Cave

Missouri on the Map

Judi and Peter are using ordered pairs to find Springfield on the map. First they find the 4, and then they go up to B. Springfield is at (4,B).

Write the city for each ordered pair.

1. (4,A) _____

2. (2,B) _____

3. (8,F) _____

4. (10,A) _____

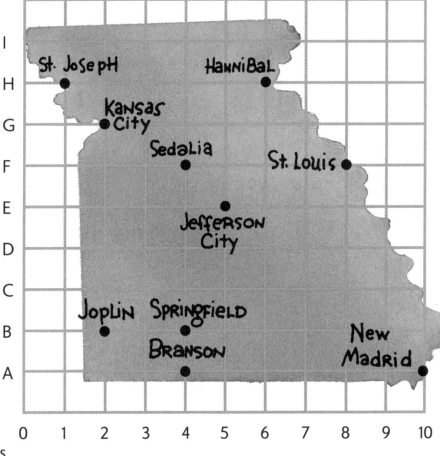

5. Give the ordered pairs for these cities.

Jefferson City: (____,____) Sedalia: (____,____) Hannibal: (____,____) St. Joseph: (____,____)

Go for It!

Look at a map of a city or state. Find five places on the map. Then write ordered pairs for their locations.

Know What?

The Gateway Arch in St. Louis was built to honor the 19th-century pioneers traveling west. The Arch is 630 feet high, 75 feet higher than the Washington Monument. 886 tons of stainless steel were needed to build the Arch.

Ordered Pairs

Going to Graceland

Graceland, in Memphis, Tennessee, was the home of the singer Elvis Presley. His home looks just like it did when Elvis lived there. You can see Elvis's cars, music awards, and grave site.

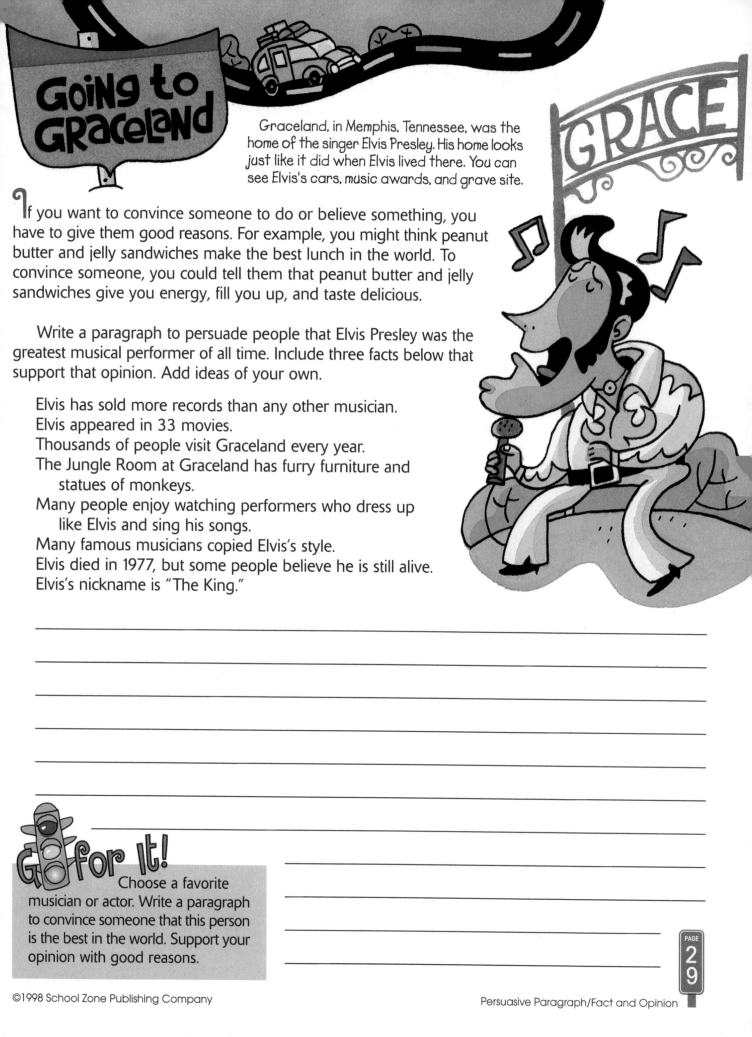

If you want to convince someone to do or believe something, you have to give them good reasons. For example, you might think peanut butter and jelly sandwiches make the best lunch in the world. To convince someone, you could tell them that peanut butter and jelly sandwiches give you energy, fill you up, and taste delicious.

Write a paragraph to persuade people that Elvis Presley was the greatest musical performer of all time. Include three facts below that support that opinion. Add ideas of your own.

Elvis has sold more records than any other musician.
Elvis appeared in 33 movies.
Thousands of people visit Graceland every year.
The Jungle Room at Graceland has furry furniture and
    statues of monkeys.
Many people enjoy watching performers who dress up
    like Elvis and sing his songs.
Many famous musicians copied Elvis's style.
Elvis died in 1977, but some people believe he is still alive.
Elvis's nickname is "The King."

_____

_____

_____

_____

_____

_____

_____

_____

_____

Go for It!

Choose a favorite musician or actor. Write a paragraph to convince someone that this person is the best in the world. Support your opinion with good reasons.

Persuasive Paragraph/Fact and Opinion

GREAT SMOKY MOUNTAINS

The Great Smoky Mountains National Park covers more than 520,000 acres and is about evenly divided between Tennessee and North Carolina.

The LaRoses are planning a route from Memphis to the Great Smoky Mountains National Park. The park has entrances at Gatlinburg, Tennessee and Cherokee, North Carolina.

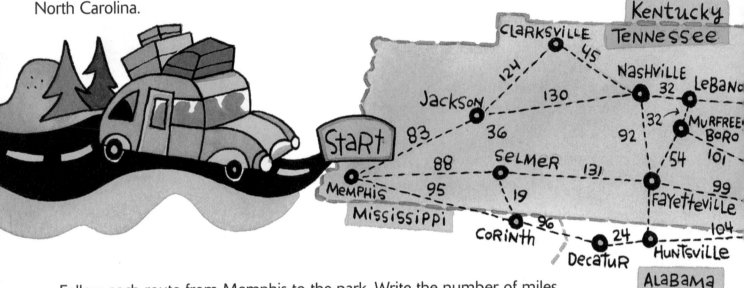

Follow each route from Memphis to the park. Write the number of miles between each pair of cities. Then calculate the total number of miles.

Memphis → Jackson → Nashville → Lebanon → Knoxville → Gatlinburg

_____ + _____ + _____ + _____ + _____ = _____

Memphis → Selmer → Fayetteville → Chattanooga → Cleveland → Cherokee

_____ + _____ + _____ + _____ + _____ = _____

Memphis → Selmer → Fayetteville → Nashville → Lebanon → Knoxville → Gatlinburg

_____ + _____ + _____ + _____ + _____ + _____ = _____

To check: Add the miles forward and backward. A calculator might help!

Know What?

The Great Smoky Mountains got their name from the blue, smokelike haze that almost always hangs over the peaks. There are 16 mountain peaks that are over 6,000 feet high and more than 200 different kinds of trees in the Great Smoky Mountains.

Equations

Find one way to get from Memphis to the park going through Murfreesboro and traveling only in Tennessee. Name the cities through which you would travel and calculate the total number of miles.

_____

_____

Find a way to get from Memphis to the park traveling through more than two states. Name the cities. Calculate the total number of miles.

_____

_____

Go for It! Make a map of a room in your house. Draw five or six objects in the room. Count the number of steps to get from one object to another. Then plan a way to touch at least three of the objects in the room and calculate the total number of steps.

KNOCK! KNOCK!

Who's there?
Shelby.
Shelby who?
Shelby comin' around the mountain when she comes...

Equations

GOLD RUSH

Dahlonega, Georgia, sits on top of the largest gold deposit east of the Mississippi River. Visitors can tour old gold mines and rent equipment to search for gold. They get to keep all the gold they find!

The past tense of most verbs is made by adding the letters -*ed* to the present tense of the verb. But irregular verbs break that rule. How do you learn irregular verbs? You memorize them.

The LaRose family is panning for gold. On each nugget, write the past tense of the verb.

LOOK

THINK   DRINK

FIND

SWING   BRING

ROW

BITE

COME

PECK

RUN   WIN

Now that you have written all the past tenses, color the nuggets with irregular verbs yellow. Which person has the most gold? _____

Go for It!

You can play Go Fish with irregular verbs. Use index cards to make your own deck. Write 26 irregular verbs and their past tense forms on separate cards. Match each verb with its past tense form to play.

Q: Why was the gold nugget sent to the loony bin?

A: He was out of his mine! (mind!)

THe Coast

Parts of the North Carolina coastline are protected in two national seashores—Cape Hatteras and Cape Lookout. Cape Hatteras has dangerous shallow waters that have caused many shipwrecks. Cape Lookout has a famous lighthouse.

The coast is the place where sea and land meet. Lighthouses let ships know where the land begins. The ocean rises at high tide and withdraws at low tide. Sand piles high on shore to form dunes and creates shallow places in the water called sand bars. Marshy areas often run along a coast.

Look at the picture. Color the different parts of the coastline this way: dunes—yellow, sand bar—tan, ocean—blue, lighthouse—red, and the area between low tide and high tide—brown.

Go for It!

Lighthouses flash their lights in special patterns to give ships information. Write a code using patterns of flashing colors. For example, red, red, long white, short white might mean "Come over and play." Share your code with a friend.

Know What?

Ocracoke Island, off the coast of North Carolina, was a hideout of the pirate Blackbeard.

Coastal Features

Key Facts

The Florida Keys are a group of small islands that stretch in a curve about 150 miles from Biscayne Bay at Miami southwest into the Gulf of Mexico. The coral reefs and sport fishing attract lots of tourists.

Write the product for each multiplication fact. Then write the products on the map to act as mile marker (MM) addresses on the islands.

COOL WORD

PRODUCT the answer to a multiplication problem

Big Pine Key	7 x 5 = _____
Grassy Key	6 x 9 = _____
Indian Key	8 x 8 = _____
Key Largo	9 x 9 = _____
Key West	7 x 0 = _____

Long Key	8 x 7 = _____
Seven Mile Bridge	6 x 7 = _____
Stock Island	3 x 4 = _____
Summerland Key	8 x 2 = _____
Windley Key	8 x 9 = _____

Go for it!

Practice the multiplication facts with a friend. See how fast you can say the 6 facts, 7 facts, 8 facts, and 9 facts.

Know What?

The only address many people have in the Florida Keys is a mile marker (MM) number. The markers are small green rectangular signs along the sides of the highway. The numbers begin with MM 126 on the Florida coast and end with MM 0 on Key West.

Multiplication Facts

Exploring Space

At the Kennedy Space Center in Florida you can learn all about the space program. You can tour a full-size model of a space shuttle, look at rockets, see movies on a screen that's five stories tall, and even watch a real space shuttle launch.

Scientists learn about space by sending space probes to fly through space or land on planets. Space probes send information back to Earth. Rovers ride around on the surface of a planet. Satellites travel around and around, or **orbit**, Earth. They are used for communication, weather forecasting, scientific research, and even spying. People ride into space on a space shuttle, where they do experiments. A space station **orbits** Earth. Astronauts may live on a space station for months at a time.

Fill in the blanks with space terms. Then write the numbered letters in the correct boxes below to discover the mystery word.

1. A space ____ __1__ ____ ____ ____ may land on a planet.

2. A ____ ____ ____ __2__ ____ ____ ____ ____ ____ travels around Earth.

3. Astronauts can live on a space __3__ ____ ____ ____ ____ ____ __4__ .

4. Astronauts ride into space and back on a space ____ ____ __5__ ____ ____ ____ ____ .

5. To ____ ____ ____ __6__ ____ means to travel around a planet.

6. A ____ ____ __7__ __8__ ____ can ride around on a planet's surface.

5	4	6	7	8	1	3	2

Go for It!

Venus is hotter than an oven, and its air is mostly poisonous gases. What if a creature could live there? Think about what that creature might look like, and then draw it.

Know What?

Space shuttles are covered with more than 24,000 tiles. These tiles protect the shuttles from temperatures higher than 3,000 degrees Fahrenheit. That's hot enough to melt steel!

Space Exploration Vocabulary

ANIMAL LOGIC

Tourists love to visit Florida's many animal parks, including Sea World, Busch Gardens, Lion Country Safari, and Parrot Jungle.

Use logic to solve these story problems about animals the LaRoses see in Florida. Read the clues. Then fill in the chart to solve the problems. Here is an example.

Peter, Judi, and Dad are watching **different** animals. Who is watching each animal?

Dad is not watching the panther.

	panther	pelican	deer
Judi			
Peter			
Dad	No		

Judi is not watching the panther either.
Peter must be watching the panther.

	panther	pelican	deer
Judi	No		
Peter	Yes		
Dad	No		

Dad is not watching the pelican.
Dad must be watching the deer.
Judi must be watching the pelican.

	panther	pelican	deer
Judi	No	Yes	No
Peter	Yes	No	No
Dad	No	No	Yes

1. Write the animal each person is watching.

Judi _____ Peter _____ Dad _____

Make up a logic problem.
Challenge a friend to solve your logic problem.

Logical Reasoning

Know What?

Marineland of Florida is the world's first oceanarium. It was built about 60 years ago on Florida's Atlantic coast between St. Augustine and Daytona Beach.

Dad, Mom, Judi, and Peter each have a **different** favorite Florida animal.
Which animal is each person's favorite? Fill in the chart completely to find out.

Judi's favorite animal is not the alligator.

Judi's favorite animal is not the manatee.

Dad's favorite animal is not the alligator
or the anhinga.

Judi's favorite animal is not the anhinga.

Peter's favorite animal is not the anhinga.

	turtle	alligator	manatee	anhinga
Judi				
Dad				
Peter				
Mom				

2. Write each person's favorite animal.

Judi _____   Dad _____

Peter _____   Mom _____

Logical Reasoning

A-Mazing Everglades

The Everglades is a huge swamp at the southern tip of Florida. The area is home to unusual plants, such as a kind of tall grass called sawgrass, and animals, including panthers, manatees, alligators, and anhingas.

The words *a*, *an*, and *the* are special adjectives called **articles**. *A* and *an* are used before nouns that name one. *A* comes before nouns that begin with a consonant sound. *An* is used before nouns that begin with a vowel sound. *The* is used both before nouns that name one and nouns that name more than one.

Help Judi and Peter find their way out of the Everglades maze. If you run into a picture that shows a noun that goes with *an*, your path is blocked. But if you run into a picture of a noun that goes with *a*, you can continue.

TiRED aLReaDY?

MosQuiTo SWaRM

Quicksand

Definite and Indefinite Articles

©1998 School Zone Publishing Company

Leech Hangout

DANGER! HUNGRY Ticks

FINISH

Quicksand

'gator graveyard

Go for It!

Play a guessing game with a friend. Take turns giving wordless clues for the nouns in the maze. See who can come up with the best clues.

KNOCK! KNOCK!

Who's there?
Everglade.
Everglade who?
Am I Everglade to see you!

Definite and Indefinite Articles

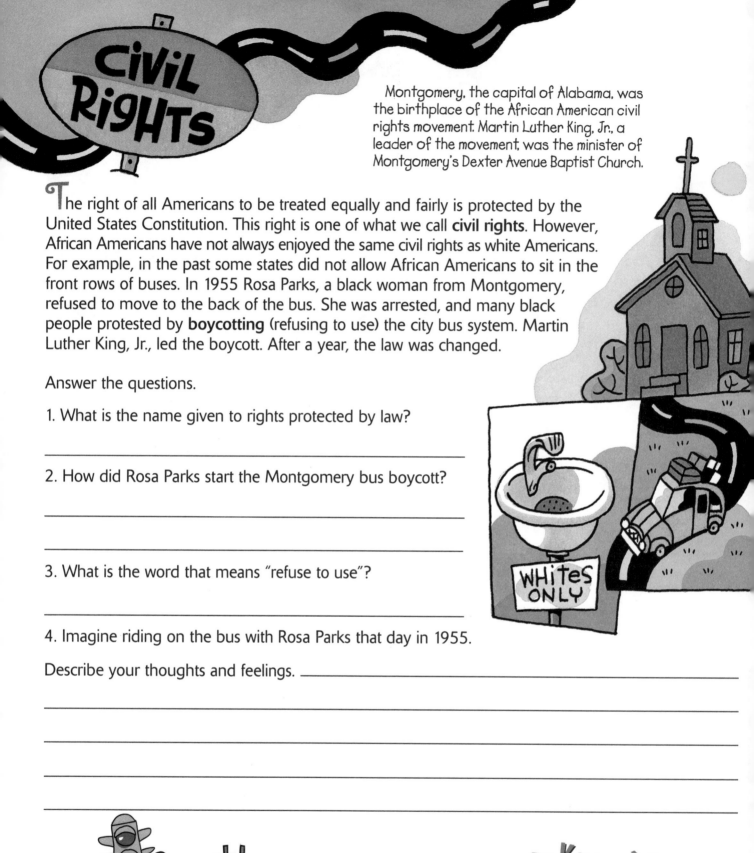

CIVIL RIGHTS

Montgomery, the capital of Alabama, was the birthplace of the African American civil rights movement. Martin Luther King, Jr., a leader of the movement, was the minister of Montgomery's Dexter Avenue Baptist Church.

The right of all Americans to be treated equally and fairly is protected by the United States Constitution. This right is one of what we call **civil rights**. However, African Americans have not always enjoyed the same civil rights as white Americans. For example, in the past some states did not allow African Americans to sit in the front rows of buses. In 1955 Rosa Parks, a black woman from Montgomery, refused to move to the back of the bus. She was arrested, and many black people protested by **boycotting** (refusing to use) the city bus system. Martin Luther King, Jr., led the boycott. After a year, the law was changed.

Answer the questions.

1. What is the name given to rights protected by law?

_____

2. How did Rosa Parks start the Montgomery bus boycott?

_____

_____

3. What is the word that means "refuse to use"?

_____

4. Imagine riding on the bus with Rosa Parks that day in 1955.

Describe your thoughts and feelings. _____

_____

_____

_____

_____

Go for It!

Take a poll. Ask neighbors or classmates which right from the constitution is most important to them. Record their responses. Make a chart listing the rights and showing the number of people who mentioned each one.

Know What?

Martin Luther King, Jr., won the 1964 Nobel Peace Prize for his leadership of the civil rights movement.

CELEBRATE!

New Orleans is an old city near the mouth of the Mississippi River. People visit New Orleans to enjoy its charming old buildings, jazz music, delicious food, and Mardi Gras celebrations.

Commas separate the parts of a sentence and help make the meaning clear. Commas are used in the following ways:

- to separate three or more items in a list: *We ate gumbo, shrimp, and hush puppies.*
- between the day and the year in a date: *February 20, 1997*
- between the city and state or city and country: *New Orleans, Louisiana, is on the Mississippi.*
- when connecting two complete sentences into one sentence using *and, or, for, nor, but, so,* or *yet*: *We went to the parade, and we saw colorful dancers.*

Add commas where they belong in the sentences.

1. Mardi Gras is an ancient festival but people still enjoy it.

2. New Orleans Louisiana has a big Mardi Gras celebration.

3. People celebrate with food music parties and parades.

4. Musicians play and colorful floats roll down the street.

5. Riders on the floats throw coins necklaces and toys.

6. The LaRose family met some people from Berlin Germany at Mardi Gras.

7. The people from Berlin spoke English so the two families enjoyed the parade together.

8. Then they went to a restaurant where they ate crayfish gumbo and jambalaya.

Go for It!

Play pin the comma on the sentence. Cut big commas from black construction paper. Write a sentence that needs commas on a large sheet of paper—but leave the commas off. Blindfold a friend and see whether your friend can put a comma in the right place.

Know What?

Mardi Gras means "fat Tuesday" in French. A long time ago, people used to parade a fat ox through French villages during Mardi Gras celebrations.

ON the GULF

Padre Island National Seashore is a sand-dune-covered barrier island that parallels the Texas coast between Port Isabel and Corpus Christi on the Gulf of Mexico.

Write the quotient for each division fact.

Cool WoRd

QUOTIENT the answer to a division problem

1. 24 ÷ 8 = ____

2. 63 ÷ 9 = ____

3. 42 ÷ 7 = ____

4. 48 ÷ 6 = ____

5. 45 ÷ 5 = ____

6. 54 ÷ 6 = ____

7. 36 ÷ 4 = ____

8. 81 ÷ 9 = ____

9. 56 ÷ 8 = ____

10. 64 ÷ 8 = ____

11. 27 ÷ 3 = ____

12. 72 ÷ 9 = ____

Go for It!

Write the division facts another way.
For example, 35 ÷ 5 = 7 can be written as $5\overline{)35}$.

Division Facts

Know What?

In some places, Padre Island is as narrow as 650 feet. In other places, it's three miles wide.

OLD MAN RIVER

The Mississippi River is sometimes called "Old Man River." It flows from a clear lake in Minnesota 2,340 miles to the Gulf of Mexico.

What should you do when you're reading and come across words you don't understand? One thing you can do is keep reading. The words around the unknown word, or the **context**, can help you. You can also get meaning clues from illustrations.

Read the paragraph and figure out what the underlined words mean. Then draw a line to match each word to its meaning.

By the time the Mississippi River reaches its southern half, tributaries such as the Arkansas River have more than doubled its amount of water. There, the river twists and winds around in loops, forming oxbow lakes. The river also deposits soil on the shore to create natural levees. The southern Mississippi River is especially important for shipping cargo. Agricultural products such as corn and wheat travel on barges pushed by tugboats.

1. tributary

2. oxbow lake

3. deposit

4. levee

5. cargo

6. agricultural

7. barge

goods shipped by boat

to dump or place

a high mound along the bank of a river

a horseshoe-shaped body of water

a large flat boat

a smaller river that flows into a larger one

made or grown on a farm

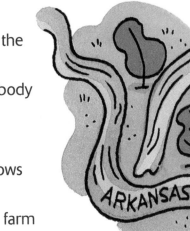

ARKANSAS RIVER

Mississippi River

G for It!

Here's a dictionary game to play with a group. Have one player find a hard word in a dictionary and write its definition. Everyone else writes made-up definitions for the word. The person who chose the word reads the actual definition and the made-up ones. Players guess which definition is real. Whoever wrote the definition that fooled the most people gets to choose the next word.

Q: Why is Old Man River so loud?

A: He has a big mouth!

Context Clues

ARE YOU MY MOM?

San Antonio, in southeastern Texas, is an important city in United States history. It is the home of a church called the Alamo. A famous battle was fought there during the war for Texas independence from Mexico.

Some animal babies look a lot like their parents. Young monkeys look like grown-up monkeys. Elephant babies do not look that different from grown-up elephants.

But some animal babies don't look at all like their parents. Young butterflies and moths are caterpillars. Young frogs are tadpoles. Young mosquitoes are little wiggly things that live in water. These animals change shape completely as they grow into adults. This change is called **metamorphosis** (meh-tuh-**morf**-uh-sihs).

Take a stroll around the San Antonio Zoo. Write the names of the adult animals and their babies. Write *m* in the boxes by the animals that change by metamorphosis.

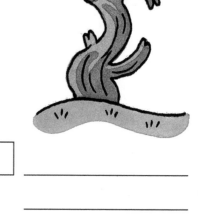

☐ _____

_____

☐ _____

_____

☐ _____

_____

☐ _____

_____

☐ _____

_____

GO for It!

Frogs go through several steps as they grow. Find out what these steps are. Draw frogs in their various stages on pieces of paper and color your drawings with bright colors. Label the steps.

Q: What did the duckling say when he saw an orange in the nest?

A: Look at the orange marmalade!

Metamorphosis

Texas Time

El Paso, the fourth largest Texas city, is in the far western part of Texas. It's so far west that it's in a different time zone from most other Texas cities!

To find elapsed time from now to a time in the future, add hours or minutes.

The time is 7:25.

In 2 hours, it will be 9:25.

In 10 minutes, it will be 9:35.

What time will it be in 3 hours?

1. _____   2. _____   3. _____

What time will it be in 20 minutes?

4. _____ 5. _____ 6. _____ 7. _____

What time will it be

in 4 hours?

in 25 minutes?

in 40 minutes?

8. _____   9. _____   10. _____

Go for It!

Make a schedule of your activities for a Saturday or a Sunday. Begin with the time you wake up. Include meal times, chores, and fun.

Q: What did the little hand say to the big hand?

A: I'll see you in an hour!

Elapsed Time

White Sands

White Sands National Monument is an area of pure-white sand dunes in southern New Mexico. The dunes are made of a mineral called gypsum, and some are more than 60 feet high.

A possessive noun shows that a person or thing owns something. Add *'s* to most singular nouns to show possession: *dog's bowl, Judi's hat*. Add *'* to most plural nouns to show possession: *parents' maps, dunes' shapes*.

Write a sentence to describe each scene from the LaRose family's day at White Sands. Use the possessive form of a noun in each sentence.

1. _____

2. _____

3. _____

4. _____

Go for It!

On a separate piece of paper, rewrite your sentences. Keep the same meaning, but don't use any possessive nouns. Can you do it?

Know What?
The state bird of New Mexico, the roadrunner, got its name because it likes to race down roads in front of cars and trucks.

Possessive Nouns

IN a CAVERN

Carlsbad Caverns National Park is a series of huge caves in southeastern New Mexico. Lighted trails display fantastic rock formations. The Caverns provide a home for more than one million Mexican free-tailed bats.

Figures are symmetric when one side matches the other side. Symmetric figures have at least one line of symmetry.

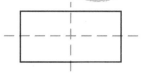

1 line of symmetry   2 lines of symmetry

Name each figure. Use the words in the box if you need help. Then draw lines of symmetry.

| octagon | circle | parallelogram | square |
| trapezoid | triangle | rectangle | pentagon |

1. _____   2. _____   3. _____   4. _____

5. _____   6. _____   7. _____   8. _____

Draw these as symmetric figures.

9. a cave entrance

10. a light bulb

Go for It!

Make several symmetric figures. Fold a piece of paper in half and cut out a design. Unfold it to see the whole figure. Also try making symmetric figures when the paper is folded twice.

Know What?

Paintings on the walls near the entrance of Carlsbad Caverns prove that Indians visited here long ago.

    Shapes and Symmetry

West Texas

West Texas is a region of dry, treeless plains and rugged mountains. It is one of the most important oil-drilling areas of the U. S. Cowboys drove their herds of cattle north through Texas. The cattle was shipped by rail to markets in the East.

Pronouns take the place of nouns.

Suzy lives in West Texas. She lives in West Texas.
The word *she* is a pronoun. *I, he, they, it, them,* and *you* are some other pronouns.

Possessive pronouns take the place of possessive nouns.

Suzy's ten-gallon hat   her ten-gallon hat
Her is a possessive pronoun. *My, his, its, our, their,* and *your* are some other possessive pronouns.

Write pronouns and possessive pronouns to take the place of the underlined words.

1. Young Pecos Bill fell from his <u>parents'</u> wagon.   _____

2. <u>Pecos Bill's</u> life changed forever.   _____

3. From then on he was the <u>coyotes'</u> child.   _____

4. The storm cloud's flood dug <u>the Grand Canyon.</u>   _____

5. <u>Pecos Bill's</u> fall made a dent called Death Valley.   _____

6. <u>Pecos Bill's sweetheart</u> was Slew Foot Sue.   _____

7. <u>Sue's</u> adventures were astonishing, too.   _____

8. <u>Mary's</u> favorite stories are tall tales.   _____

Go for It!

Many tall tales are fun stories that give impossible explanations for how real things came to be. Think about something in nature. Then write a tall tale to explain it.

Know What?

People sometimes call cowboys "cowpokes" because cowboys used to poke cattle with sticks when they loaded the cattle onto train cars.

Pronouns and Possessive Pronouns

SOUTHWESTERN SHAPES

Native American, Mexican, and Anglo people live in Santa Fe, the capital of New Mexico. The Plaza, a square block in the middle of the city, has been an important center of commerce, festivals, and history for more than 400 years.

A figure can be moved in many ways. You can make interesting geometric patterns with shapes and moves. Lots of Native American art has patterns made by using this method.

 slide

slide   flip   turn

Write the word *slide*, *flip*, or *turn* to explain how to get each dark figure.

1. _____   2. _____   3. _____   4. _____

Look at each pattern. Draw and color the next figure. Write *slide*, *flip*, or *turn* in the blank to show what you did.

5.

_____

6.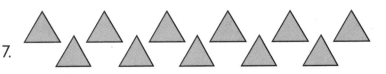

_____

7.

_____

8.

_____

 **for It!**

Design a T-shirt with a pattern. Use a geometric shape with slides, turns, or flips. Color your design.

Know What?

The state capitol of New Mexico has a round design that resembles the Zia sun symbol, the official emblem of the state.

Geometrical Patterns

PUEBLO INDIANS

You can see ruins of cliff dwellings in Mesa Verde National Park in southern Colorado. Ancient Indians built these dwellings on ledges of high cliffs. Some are like apartment buildings. One has more than 200 rooms.

Some Pueblo Indians live in villages called **pueblos** (**pweb**-lohz) in New Mexico and Arizona. Many of their houses are similar to the cliff dwellings at Mesa Verde. Many pueblo dwellers follow their old ways of life and religion. They hold religious ceremonies in underground rooms called **kivas** (**kee**-vuhz). The Pueblo people make beautiful pottery and baskets.

Use the clues to fill in the words in the puzzle.

Across

1. Pueblo Indians make beautiful _____ and baskets.

4. A _____ is an underground room.

5. A flat-topped hill is called a _____ .

7. Many Pueblos are in New _____ .

Down

1. Another name for a village is _____ .

2. Some cliff dwellings have many _____ .

3. *Mesa* is the Spanish word for _____ .

6. Ancient Indians built _____ dwellings.

GO for It!

Dancing is important to many Native Americans. Make up a dance to express something about yourself or how you feel. Perform the dance for someone.

Know What?

Mesa means "table" in Spanish, and *verde* means "green." Spanish-speaking people named the flat-topped hills of the Southwestern United States *mesas* because they look like giant tables. Why do you think they called the hills *verde*?

Pueblo Indians

Desert Crawlers

Deserts cover much of the southern half of Utah. There, the wind has carved the sandstone into wondrous towers and arches. The water in the Great Salt Lake in northern Utah is saltier than the ocean.

The desert is a harsh place, but many insects and spiders are right at home there.

- The thistledown velvet ant is actually a wingless wasp that lives in the sand. Its brown body is covered with white hairs, so it looks like a cotton ball. It feeds on nectar.
- Wind scorpions are yellowish-brown and about an inch long. They catch insects, lizards, and other small animals with their large pincers.
- The trapdoor spider digs a silk-lined burrow in the sand up to a foot deep. It makes a trap door with a hinge of silk. It lies in wait in its burrow and grabs passing insects.
- The black cactus longhorn beetle is shiny and black with long feelers. It grows up to about an inch long and eats cactus.

Below are drawings of parts of the creatures described. Figure out which bug each part belongs to. Write the name of the creatures on the lines.

1. _____

2. _____

3. _____

_____

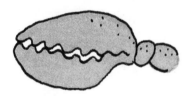

4. _____

5. _____

6. _____

_____

Go for It!

Insects are everywhere. If it's the right time of year, find an insect or spider to observe. It could be an ant gathering food, a spider spinning a web, or a bee visiting flowers. Write or draw your observations.

Know What?

Tarantulas got their name from a type of spider found near Taranto, Italy. People used to believe that this spider's bite made people leap in the air and make weird noises. They thought that doing a dance called the tarantella cured the sickness.

Desert Animals

It's a Grand Canyon

The Grand Canyon in northwestern Arizona is 277 miles long and a mile deep. The Colorado River carved the canyon through layers of colorful stone. Many visitors ride mules to the bottom of the canyon.

The words *it's* and *its* look similar, but they have very different meanings. *Its* is a possessive pronoun. *Its* takes the place of a noun that names an object or an animal: *Its hair grew six inches last summer.*

It's is a contraction for the words *it is*: *It's not my fault!* A contraction is a short form of two words. A letter or letters are left out and an apostrophe takes their place.

Circle the correct word to complete each sentence.

1. Dad said, "It's Its time to get up."

2. "It's Its too early," Peter mumbled.

3. "It's Its a great day for a mule ride!" Dad replied.

4. Judi gave her mule it's its breakfast.

5. "Do you think it's its going to rain?" asked Mom.

6. Peter saw a lizard that had lost it's its tail.

7. "Look at the squirrel with it's its furry ears," said Judi.

8. "It's Its a different color from squirrels at home," she added.

Go for It!

Go on an "*it's/its* patrol." As you read signs, directions, or newspapers, be on the lookout for *it's/its* mix-ups. You'll be surprised how many you find.

Q. How much dirt is there in a hole 10 feet by 10 feet?

A. None! (There's no dirt in a hole.)

It's and Its

How Hot?

Death Valley is a deep trough in east-central California. The lowest part, 282 feet, is near Badwater. The highest temperature ever recorded in the United States, 134° F, was reported there in 1913.

You can use a Fahrenheit thermometer to measure temperature. The one at the right shows some temperatures to remember.

Write the temperatures in degrees Fahrenheit.

1. _____   2. _____   3. _____   4. _____

°F

212°F WATER BOILS

Hot Cocoa

98.6 °F NORMAL BODY TEMPERATURE

ROOM TEMPERATURE

COLD WATER

32°F WATER FREEZES

Look at the temperatures. Which is the most reasonable for each picture? Write the temperature under each picture.

| 18° F | 59° F |
| 80° F | 101° F |

5. _____   6. _____   7. _____   8. _____

Go for It!

Write a letter to someone who lives in a different climate from yours. Discuss the seasons: what the weather is like, what clothing you need, which activities are fun.

Know What?

The average rainfall on the floor of Death Valley is less than 2 inches per year!

PAGE 53

Thermometer

City By the Bay

San Francisco's many attractions include Golden Gate Park, Chinatown, and Fisherman's Wharf. Visitors enjoy views of twinkling ocean waters from atop tall hills. They love the cable cars that chug up and down steep, narrow streets.

When we read, we often come across statements that are facts. Facts can be proved: *San Francisco is in California.* We also read opinions: *San Francisco is the most beautiful city in California.* Opinions can't be proved.

Tour the city with the LaRose family. They'll hear some information from the tour guide. Write *f* next to those that are facts. Write *o* next to the statements that are opinions. Write *f + o* next to those that contain facts and opinions.

1. The best seafood restaurant is Wing Chun, which is in Chinatown.

_____

2. Chinatown is in the northeast corner of the city.

_____

3. Wing Chun is owned by my uncle.

_____

4. You will be disappointed if you do not eat at Wing Chun.

_____

5. Wing Chun has a team of master chefs trained in China.

_____

6. At Wing Chun, you have a choice of hot, medium, or mild sauce, but the hot sauce is the tastiest.

_____

7. Wing Chun serves forty-two types of shrimp dumplings.

_____

8. No dish on the menu costs more than $8.95.

_____

9. My cousin will offer you a mint as you leave.

_____

10. Wing Chun is a real bargain!

_____

Go for It!

In your opinion, did the LaRose family learn much about Chinatown on their tour? On a separate piece of paper, explain why or why not.

Know What?

Lombard Street in San Francisco is called the most crooked street in the world. In just one steep block, Lombard makes eight sharp turns.

Fact and Opinion

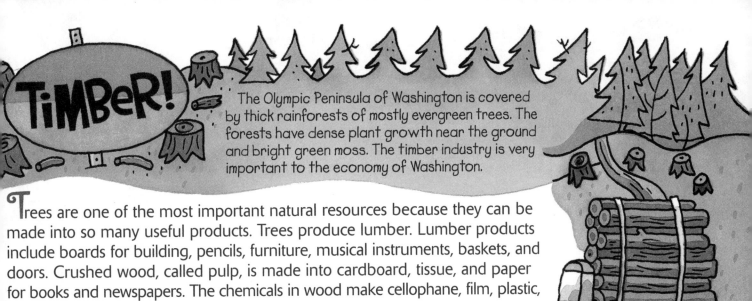

TiMBeR!

The Olympic Peninsula of Washington is covered by thick rainforests of mostly evergreen trees. The forests have dense plant growth near the ground and bright green moss. The timber industry is very important to the economy of Washington.

Trees are one of the most important natural resources because they can be made into so many useful products. Trees produce lumber. Lumber products include boards for building, pencils, furniture, musical instruments, baskets, and doors. Crushed wood, called pulp, is made into cardboard, tissue, and paper for books and newspapers. The chemicals in wood make cellophane, film, plastic, ink, paint, dye, cloth, and cement.

Below are some products made from trees. Write the name of each product in the correct column.

Lumber					
Pulp					
Chemicals					

Go for It!

Think of a product or service you could offer people. What would you call your business? How much would you charge? How would you let people know about your business? Write your ideas.

Q. How do trees celebrate a birthday?

A: They throw a lumber party!

Products from Trees

Write on Home

The LaRose family is finally back at home in Seattle after their vacation. Have you learned a lot and enjoyed the trip as much as they have?

A paragraph is a group of sentences about one idea. Often the first sentence is a topic sentence that tells what the paragraph is about. The first sentence is indented. Supporting sentences give more information, or support, the topic sentence. Often a conclusion sums up the paragraph.

Write a paragraph about home. It can be about your town, your house, your family, or a place you would like to live. Make sure the paragraph has the three parts described above.

LaRose

_____

_____

_____

_____

_____

_____

_____

_____

_____

Go for It!

Did you smile at the riddles in the book? Try writing some riddles of your own—the sillier the better!

Parts of a Paragraph

Language Arts

Activities to Share

Though by third grade most children are reading independently, that's no reason to stop reading aloud to your child. Reading and talking about books you read together are wonderful ways to develop your child's language arts skills—reading, writing, listening, and speaking. Show your child you value reading by taking time to read yourself. Talk about what you're reading, too.

Be on the lookout for opportunities in your daily routine to read and write with your child. Write shopping lists together. At the grocery store, read signs and food labels. Ask your child to read signs and billboards. As you work in the kitchen, encourage your child to read recipes with you, and when assembling a toy or using an appliance for the first time, have your child help you read and follow the directions.

The New Read-Aloud Handbook by Jim Trelease provides dos and don'ts for reading aloud and pointers for encouraging independent reading. An extensive bibliography of books organized by difficulty level is included to help you choose books to read to your child.

Another book with tips and strategies for enhancing your child's appreciation of reading is *Story Stretchers for the Primary Grades: Activities to Expand Children's Favorite Books* by Shirley C. Raines and Robert J. Canady. A companion book, *450 More Story Stretchers* by Shirley C. Raines, picks up where the 1992 book left off.

The United States Department of Education's Web site has many tips for enhancing your child's language skills. Visit these two sites: www.ed.gov/pubs/parents/Reading and www.ed.gov/pubs/parents/Writing.

Here are some additional language arts activities for you and your child.

Word Chains and Circles Give your child a word, and then have him or her change the word into a different word by changing a single letter. For example: *cane, cone; done, dome; dime, dire; tire, tore.* Encourage your child to make a long chain.

Compound Word Chains Start your child out with a compound word. Then challenge the child to make a chain of compound words by changing one word of the compound at a time, for example *honeybee, beekeeper, housekeeper, treehouse, treetop, tophat.*

Draw the Idioms Explain that English has many expressions that mean something very different from the meanings of the individual words. Give examples, such as *He was flat broke, She threw caution to the winds,* or *He is beside himself with anger.* Think of some familiar idioms together and encourage your child to draw the literal meanings of the expressions.

Postcards Postcards aren't just for vacations. Buy postcards or have your child make some of heavy postcard stock cut to standard size. Show your child where to write the salutation, date, address, body, closing, and signature. Encourage your child to write to relatives and friends close to home or far away. Everyone loves to get postcards. Encourage grandparents and other relatives to send postcards and letters to your child. Letters and E-mail are fun to send and receive, too.

Story in a Box Fill a shoebox with a number of small, interesting items, such as figurines, tickets, natural objects, and so on. Have your child reach in and pull out three items. Ask your child to study the items and write a story that includes all three.

 # Activities to Share

In 1989, the National Council of Teachers of Mathematics (NCTM) developed the Curriculum and Evaluation Standards for School Mathematics. These standards specify that the mathematics curriculum should emphasize problem solving, using reasoning skills, communicating about mathematics, and making connections among math topics. It also specifies that children should learn to value mathematics and become confident in their own abilities. The NCTM advises that children have hands-on and varied experiences; use manipulatives, calculators, and computers; and work in pairs or cooperative groups. The NCTM wants children to "do" math, "make sense" of math, and "connect" math to real life to develop the skills necessary to function in today's society.

At home, you can help your child accomplish the NCTM goals. Here are some ways to follow up the math activities in this book and nurture a curiosity for mathematical ideas.

Follow Up the Lessons. Follow up the math lessons in this book by asking similar questions or thinking of similar problems. Urge your child to talk about mathematics to develop communication skills. Also ask how math lessons in school are similar to the activities you share at home.

Keep a Math Journal. Have your child record math vocabulary words as they appear in the lessons. Review these words from time to time. Have him or her record interesting problems and puzzles, as well as ways math is used at home, in stores, and in the neighborhood. Take the journal on trips so your child can make entries about numbers on signs or buildings, record license plate numbers, write down times and temperatures, make a list of words from the word *mathematics,* or figure out how many ways a number can be written (e.g., 10: 4 + 6, 3 + 3 + 2 + 2, 2 x 3 + 4). Many of the Go for It! extension activities can be written in the math journal.

Do Math Every Day. Nurture your child's curiosity by asking a math question every day. Ask your child to help you figure out an answer to a real-life problem, such as finding the best buy or measuring something. Ask him or her about shapes in nature and man-made things, such as boxes or buildings. Plan periodic "scavenger hunts" to look for mathematics in the home, at an event, or in the park. Involve other members of the family, friends, or neighbors occasionally to work cooperatively towards a solution.

Follow a Recipe. This is an enjoyable way for your child to practice using fractions. Challenge your child to double or halve a recipe. Use measuring cups and spoons. Help your child learn how many ounces are in a cup, how many cups are in a quart, and how many quarts are in a gallon.

Develop Problem Solving Skills. Have counters handy to help your child to figure out computational problems if multiplication facts or addition skills are not recalled easily. Use common objects found in the home, such as coins, straws, or buttons. Also help your child realize that there may be many ways to solve a problem, and that some problems may have more than one solution. When your child makes a mistake, analyze the approach and information used. Making mistakes can be another way of learning new ideas. Help your child develop ways to become an independent problem solver and rely on his or her knowledge and abilities.

Activities to Share

You and your child will enjoy these hands-on science activities. You will find that science skills, such as predicting, observing, measuring, classifying, analyzing, and evaluating, come naturally as your child's innate curiosity about the world and how it works is engaged.

There are a number of excellent books of science projects for children. Janice VanCleave is the author of numerous books of this type. Also try *Creepy Crawlies and the Scientific Method: Over 100 Hands-on Science Experiments for Children* by Sally Stenhouse Kneidel, *Science Around the House* by Robert Gardner, and *Teach Your Child Science: Making Science Fun for Both of You* by Michael Shermer.

The United States Department of Education's Web site has many tips for enhancing your child's science skills. Visit this site: www.ed.gov/pubs/parents/science.

The **physical science** concept of buoyancy taught in this book is easy to demonstrate at home. Float margarine or yogurt containers in a basin of water. Add objects to them until they sink, and then weigh the objects. Explore reasons why it took different amounts of weight to sink different containers. Or fill a basin with water to the very top. Place the basin in another, empty, basin. Put a solid object in the first basin so that some of the water overflows. Measure the volume of water that is displaced by the object. Explain that the weight of this volume of water equals the buoyancy of the water. See *The Way Things Work* by David Macaulay.

Extend the **natural sciences** concepts in this book by observing nature with your child. With your child, examine a flower's parts. Using the diagram in the book, identify the parts. Look at flowers gone to seed and flowers that have changed into fruit. Explain that fruits are one way that plants spread their seeds so that new plants can grow. Find out together the role that insects play in the development of seeds. See *The Clover and the Bee: A Book of Pollination* and *From Flower to Fruit* both by Anne O. Dowden.

Earth and space sciences can be as close as your backyard. Your child learned about satellites and other space devices in this book. If you live in an area without too much light, you can see satellites almost any night. On a dark, clear night, look for starlike points of light that move very slowly in a straight line across the sky. If they look too small to be airplanes, they are likely to be satellites. See *Spacecraft Technology* by John Mason for an illustrated overview of the machines used to explore space.

Explain that soil is ground-up rocks and minerals mixed with decayed plant material. Find out what kind of soil is most common in the area where you live. If you have a garden, show your child how you enrich the soil. Encourage your child to help you with planting, weeding, and other gardening tasks. See *The Field Guide to Geology* by David Lambert and the Diagram Group and *A Shovelful of Earth* by Lorus J. and Margery Milne.

It is especially important to put the concept of **nutrition** into practice in everyday life. Help your child plan a meal. Make a chart with spaces for protein, fiber, starch, and fat. Allow your child to fill out the chart with a favorite food from each category. As long as the choices create a balanced meal, let your child choose a family dinner. See *Foodworks: Over 100 Science Activities and Fascinating Facts That Explore the Magic of Food* by the Ontario Science Centre and *Eat the Right Stuff* by Catherine Reef.

SOCIAL STUDIES Activities to Share

The social studies range from geography to history, from economics to citizenship and government. Generally speaking, they are the study of how people relate to their environment and to one another.

The United States Department of Education's Web site has many tips for enhancing your child's social studies skills. Visit this site: www.ed.gov/pubs/parents/geography.

You can make **geography** and **regional studies** meaningful to your child by relating them to your own home and community. Talk about your town and the types of houses people live in there. If you live in a region where the winters are cold, point out how the homes are built to be warm in the winter. If you live in a warm climate, explain to your child that your home has features that help it stay cool. Ask your child to imagine what it would be like to live in a different climate. See *Science for Kids: 39 Easy Geography Activities* by Robert W. Wood, *Exploring Your World: The Adventures of Geography*, and *The National Geographic Society Picture Atlas of Our Fifty States*.

You have many opportunities to teach your child **map skills**. Together, you can draw a map of your house showing your escape plan in case of fire or another emergency. You can also involve your child in planning a route for a trip. Study a map together and discuss the various symbols. Show your child the route you intend to take.

Being aware of how we use and protect **natural resources** is becoming increasingly important as the population grows and resources become more scarce. If you have a good-sized yard, you and your child can make your own small "national park." Set aside an area that you will allow to grow naturally. If you live in the plains, your national park may become a prairie. If you live in a desert climate, very little may grow there. Observe your national park to see if any animals move in. If they do, observe them carefully so you don't disturb them. See *Land Use and Abuse* by D. J. Herda and Margaret L. Madden and *50 Simple Things Kids Can Do to Save the Earth* by The Earthworks Group.

Many youngsters are fascinated with the culture and history of **Native Americans**. You and your child will enjoy making—and eating—this Native American fried bread.
Ingredients:

2 1/2 cups flour	1 tsp. salt	3/4 cup warm water
1 1/2 tbs. baking powder	1 tbs. dried skim milk	1 tbs. vegetable oil

Mix the flour, baking powder, and salt in a large bowl. Mix the powdered milk, water, and vegetable oil in a small bowl. Mix the liquid with the dry ingredients and stir until the dough is smooth. Knead the dough for 30 seconds. Cover it with a cloth and let it sit 10 minutes. Divide the dough in half, and keep dividing each piece in half until you have 8 pieces. Roll each piece of dough into a circle 8 to 10 inches across. In a large frying pan, heat about 1 inch of vegetable oil. Fry each circle of dough until golden brown. Drain on paper towels. Serve the bread hot.

No matter what your racial or ethnic background, the struggle for **civil rights** will move and interest your child. Encourage your child to discuss what equality means to him or her. Ask whether your child has ever seen someone being treated unfairly. What happened? Why was it unfair? See *Martin Luther King, Jr.: Dreams for a Nation* by Louise Quayle and *The Great Migration: An American Story* by Jacob Lawrence.

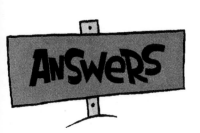

ANSWERS

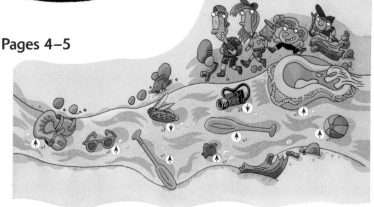

Page 2
1. sentence
2. not a sentence
3. sentence
4. sentence
5. not a sentence
6. not a sentence
7. not a sentence
8. sentence
9. sentence
10. not a sentence

Page 3
1. $27 > $19
2. $31 > $27
3. $87 < $89
4. $68 < $79
5. $127 > $108
6. Spokane Supermart
7. $18

Pages 4–5

Dad's sunglasses float because their density is less than the density of water.

Page 6
1. 40 + 8
2. 100 + 20 + 0
3. 100 + 20 + 5
4. 200 + 30 + 6
5. 70 + 9
6. 200 + 60 + 1
7. 400 + 30 + 5
8. 300 + 70 + 2
9. 300 + 0 + 3
10. 100 + 90 + 7

Page 7
Answers will vary. Places should be named and described. Three reasons for protecting the places should be listed.

Page 8
O = 37 U = 41 T = 104
S = 114 R = 36 E = 79 N = 89 H = 17 M = 66

MOUNT RUSHMORE

Page 9
Verbs: shines, grow, attack, gobble
Nouns: park, sun, trees, ladybugs
Adjectives: big, tall, harmful
Adverbs: brightly, quickly

Page 10
1. 9
2. 17
3. 2
4. 86
5. 158
6. 119
7. 54
8. 8
9. 3

Page 11
1. fiber
2. fiber
3. protein
4. starch
5. protein
6. fat

Pages 12–13

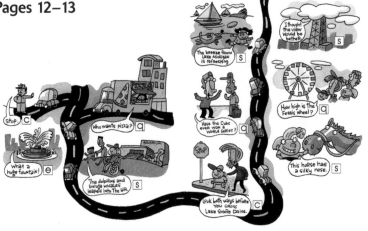

Page 14

Page 15
The Stars of football shine at the Pro Football Hall of Fame in canton, ohio. the Hall of Fame opened on september 7, 1963. Every year, the league names a few of its Best players to the Hall of Fame. there, visitors can See pictures of these players, their Uniforms, and their equipment.

Page 16
1. 2
2. Grand Island
3. about 4 miles
4. city
5. 2
6. Lake Erie, Lake Ontario

Page 17
1. opened
2. use
3. closes
4. continue
5. constructed
6. will read

Page 18

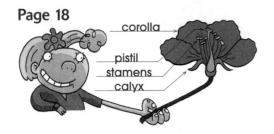

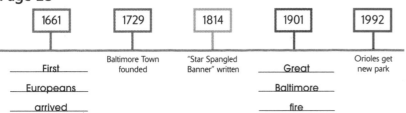

corolla

pistil
stamens
calyx

New plants grow from seeds.

Page 19

6
1
3
2
5
4
7

Page 20

__3__ Chrysler Building, 77 stories   1,250 feet

__5__ Citicorp Center, 59 stories   915 feet

__2__ Empire State Building, 102 stories   1,377 feet

__4__ RCA Building, 70 stories   850 feet

__1__ World Trade Center, 110 stories   1,046 feet

527 feet taller

Page 21

1. Brooklyn 3,455 feet
2. Verrazano-Narrows 6,690 feet
3. Williamsburg 2,793 feet
4. Queensboro 3,724 feet
5. George Washington 4,760 feet

Page 22

1. The Pretzel Museum is open from Mon. through Sat. from 9 a.m. to 5 p.m.
2. Its address is 211 North Third St., Philadelphia.
3. Mr. LaRose ate six pretzels.
4. America's first pretzel bakery opened in Lititz, Penn. in 1861.
5. The LaRose family saw a 7-min. movie on pretzels.
6. They bought a box of pretzels for their friend, Dr. Banks.

Page 23

| 1661 | 1729 | 1814 | 1901 | 1992 |

First   Baltimore Town founded   "Star Spangled Banner" written   Great   Orioles get new park

Europeans   Baltimore

arrived   fire

Pages 24–25

1. antonyms
2. homophones
3. synonyms
4. antonyms
5. homophones
6. homophones
7. synonyms
8. synonyms
9. antonyms
10. antonyms

Page 26

1. 34   2. 52   3. 205
4. 538   5. 305   6. 797
7. 298   8. 326

Know What?
George Washington, Thomas Jefferson, James Madison, James Monroe, William Henry Harrison, John Tyler, Zachary Taylor, Woodrow Wilson

Page 27

column

chamber

stalactite

stalagmite

Page 28

1. Branson
2. Joplin
3. St. Louis
4. New Madrid

5. (5,E) (4,F) (6,H) (1,H)

Page 29

Paragraphs will vary, but should include three facts from this page.

Pages 30–31

83 + 130 + 32 + 146 + 38 = 429 miles
88 + 131 + 99 + 30 + 119 = 467 miles
88 + 131 + 92 + 32 + 146 + 38 = 527 miles

Answers will vary. One possibility is:
Memphis → Selmer → Fayetteville → Murfreesboro → Lebanon → Knoxville → Gatlinburg:
88 + 131 + 54 + 32 + 146 + 38 = 489 miles

Answers will vary. One possibility is:
Memphis → Corinth → Decatur → Huntsville → Chattanooga → Cleveland → Cherokee:
95 + 96 + 24 + 104 + 30 + 119 = 468 miles

Page 32

looked,
thought, drank

found,
swung, brought

rowed,
bit, came

pecked,
ran, won

Peter

Page 33

Page 34

Big Pine Key = 35   Long Key = 56
Grassy Key = 54   Seven Mile Bridge = 42
Indian Key = 64   Stock Island = 12
Key Largo = 81   Summerland Key = 16
Key West = 0   Windley Key = 72

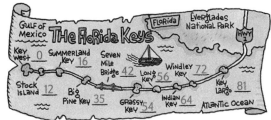

Page 35

1. probe
2. satellite
3. station
4. shuttle
5. orbit
6. rover

universe

Pages 36–37

1. pelican, panther, deer

2. turtle, manatee,
   alligator, anhinga

Pages 38–39

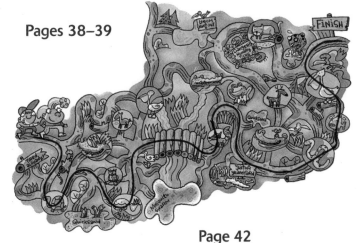

Page 40

1. civil rights
2. She refused to move
   to the back of the bus.
3. boycott
4. Answers will vary.

Page 41

1. Mardi Gras is an ancient festival, but people still enjoy it.
2. New Orleans, Louisiana, has a big Mardi Gras celebration.
3. People celebrate with food, music, parties, and parades.
4. Musicians play, and colorful floats roll down the street.
5. Riders on the floats throw coins, necklaces, and toys.
6. The LaRose family met some people from Berlin, Germany,
   at Mardi Gras.
7. The people from Berlin spoke English, so the two families
   enjoyed the parade together.
8. Then they went to a restaurant where they ate crayfish,
   gumbo, and jambalaya.

Page 42

1. 3		2. 7
3. 6	4. 8	5. 9
6. 9	7. 9	8. 9
9. 7	10. 8	11. 9	12. 8

Page 43

1. tributary — a smaller river that flows into a larger one
2. oxbow lake — a horseshoe-shaped body of water
3. deposit — to dump or place
4. levee — a high mound along the bank of a river
5. cargo — goods shipped by boat
6. agricultural — made or grown on a farm
7. barge — a large flat boat

Page 44

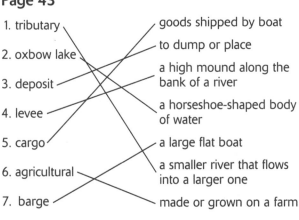

duck   goose   [m]
duckling OR gosling

frog
tadpole

deer
fawn

bear
cub

[m] butterfly
caterpillar

Answers

Page 45
1. 10:25   2. 7:40   3. 1:00
4. 6:30   5. 9:25   6. 3:05   7. 4:10
8. 10:30   9. 10:55   10. 2:55

Page 46
Answers will vary. Possible sentences include
1. Dad's van had a flat tire.
2. Peter's canteen is leaking.
3. The kites' tails are long and colorful.
4. Judi saw a lizard's footprints.

Page 47
1. trapezoid - 1 line
2. rectangle - 2 lines
3. circle - many lines
4. pentagon - 1 line
5. triangle - 1 line
6. parallelogram - no lines
7. square - 2 lines
8. octagon - 2 lines
9.    10.

Page 48
1. their
2. His
3. their
4. it
5. His
6. She
7. Her
8. Her

Page 49
1. flip
2. slide
3. turn
4. flip
5. turn
6. flip
7. slide
8. flip

Page 50

Page 51
1. wind scorpion
2. black cactus longhorn beetle
3. trapdoor spider
4. wind scorpion
5. thistledown velvet ant
6. black cactus longhorn beetle

Page 52
1. It's
2. It's
3. It's
4. its
5. it's
6. its
7. its
8. It's

Page 53
1. 78° F   2. 20° F   3. 92° F   4. 53° F

5. 101° F   6. 18° F   7. 59° F   8. 80° F

Page 54
1. f + o   2. f   3. f   4. o
5. f   6. f + o   7. f
8. f   9. f   10. o

Page 55
Lumber: instrument, telephone pole
Pulp: bag, tissue, book
Chemicals: ink, shirt, film, paint, cement block

Page 56
Paragraphs will vary, but should include a topic sentence, supporting details, and conclusion.